W9-BEZ-030

Scripture quotations identified KJV are from the King James Version of the Bible.

Scripture quotations identified TLB are taken from The Living Bible, copyright © 1971 by Tyndale House Publishers, Wheaton, IL. Used by permission.

Scripture quotations identified NIV are taken from the HOLY BIBLE: NEW INTER- NATIONAL VERSION Copyright © 1978 by the New York International Bible Society. Used by permission of Zondervan Bible Publishers.

Scripture quotations identified NAS are from the New American Standard Bible, Copyright © THE LOCKMAN FOUNDATION 1960, 1962, 1963, 1968, 1971, 1972, 1973, 1975, 1977 and are used by permission.

"Sheer Joy" by Ralph Spaulding Cushman quoted from SPIRITUAL HILLTOPS, published by Abingdon Press. Used by permission of the publisher.

Quotation from the book *Parables by the Sea* by Pamela Reeve, copyright 1976, Multnomah Press, Portland, Oregon 97266. Used by permission.

Quotation from THE KING AND I
Copyright © 1951 by Richard Rodgers and Oscar Hammerstein
Williamson Music Co., owner of publication and allied rights throughout the
Western Hemisphere and Japan.
International Copyright Secured.
ALL RIGHTS RESERVED. Used by permission.

Quotation from THE SOUND OF MUSIC
Copyright © 1959 by Richard Rodgers and Oscar Hammerstein
Williamson Music Co., owner of publication and allied rights throughout the
Western Hemisphere and Japan.
International Copyright Secured.
ALL RIGHTS RESERVED. Used by permission.

Quotation reprinted from *God Is a Verb* by Marilee Zdenek and Marge Champion, copyright © 1974; used by permission of Word Books Publishers, Waco, Texas 76796.

ISBN 0-8007-1374-5

Copyright © 1984 by Cassandre Maxwell
Published by Fleming H. Revell Company
All rights reserved
Printed in the United States of America

A Legacy for My Loved Ones

Cassandre Maxwell

Calligraphy by Eve Polston

Fleming H. Revell Company
Old Tappan, New Jersey

Contents

Introduction

Frank and Clara Edelman celebrated sixty-seven years of life together. In that time, they experienced the joys of buying their own home and raising a child. They lived through two world wars, a flood, and the "flu of 1918," which claimed the lives of half the people in their town. They helped their neighbors, went to picnics and camp meetings, and faithfully attended their church. In their later years they buried many of their loved ones, often after nursing them through long illnesses. Frank also changed careers, becoming an automobile mechanic after blacksmiths were rarely needed. When they were young, they traveled by "horse 'n buggy"; their grandchildren travel by jet plane. In their lifetime they routinely did things people rarely do today, such as making their own soap and butchering their own animals for meat, preserving it very successfully without refrigeration.

Hearing their stories gives one a living sense of history—a legacy, so to speak. Being part of their family gave me knowledge of where I had come from and challenge and comfort for where I am going.

This book is dedicated to them; but it is also dedicated to all those who take time to pass on *their* legacies to *their* loved ones.

Introduction

Have you ever come across old postcards or letters written many years before? They always hold a fascination for us, help us remember a time past, and reveal something of the personality of the writer. What we take time to write down often holds tremendous significance later on!

The themes of remembering and being thankful are very important ones in the Bible. Over and over again, God's people are commanded to remember His provision, guidance, and love for them *and* to thank Him. One of the best ways we can do this is to write down how God has led us. Those who follow us are sure to have their lives blessed and their faith strengthened if they can read about God's faithfulness in the past.

A Legacy for My Loved Ones is designed to help you record a lifetime of thoughts and experiences. "Milestones" provides a summary of the highlights of your life; "Favorites" and "Firsts" are sections youngsters will easily relate to; the other sections provide an in-depth look at you, your life, and your hope for the life to come. The verses, pictures, and poems will inspire you along the way.

We are told in the book of Malachi, that those who reverence the Lord and "love to think about him, have their names recorded in *His* 'Book of Remembrance'" (*see* Malachi 3:16). What a wonderful thought! God writes down our names and remembers us, too!

Milestones
"Getting to know you..."

Name: _____

Birth date: _____

Place and time you were born: _____

Name of the president of the United States then: _____

Present address and phone number:

_____

_____

Physical description (including adult height, weight, eye and hair color):

_____

_____

_____

O Lord, you have searched me and you know me. You know when I sit and when I rise; you perceive my thoughts from afar.

Your background nationality: _____

The date you were baptized (or dedicated) and the place: _____

_____

The towns or cities in which you lived while you were growing up: _____

_____

_____

_____

Your church affiliation then: _____

_____

Date and age you were confirmed or joined the church: _____

You discern my going out and my lying
down; you are familiar with all my ways.
Psalms 139: 1-3 NIV

Schooling

Date you started school: _____

Names of elementary and high schools: Date(s) of graduation:

_____   _____

_____

_____   _____

_____

Special recognition (honors or awards you received):

_____

_____

Any higher education you received: Date(s) of graduation: Degree(s) held:

_____   _____   _____

_____   _____   _____

Special honors or awards you received:

_____

_____

Organizations to which you belonged:

_____

_____

_____

Before a word is on my tongue you
know it completely, O Lord.

12

Life Work

What did you do when you went to work?

_____

_____

_____

_____

Or was your work centered in your home (keeping house, raising a family)?

_____

Over the years, what were some of the different jobs you held?

_____

_____

_____

_____

_____

...you created my inmost being; you knit me together in my mother's womb.
Psalms 139: 4, 13 NIV

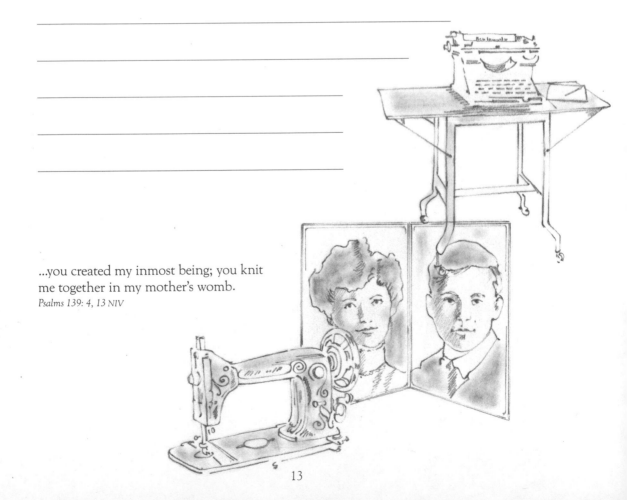

13

Your Marriage

Date of your marriage: _____

Name and physical description of your spouse: _____
_____

The towns and cities where you lived together: _____
_____
_____

Your children's names and birth dates: _____
_____
_____
_____

Your church affiliation while your children were growing up: _____
_____

Date of your retirement: _____

Hobbies and activities pursued during retirement:
_____
_____
_____
_____

I praise you because
I am fearfully and wonderfully made....

The things you were known for during your lifetime:
Your special talents and abilities _____

_____

_____

_____

Any sports in which you excelled _____

_____

_____

_____

Any musical instruments that you played _____

_____

_____

_____

Any foreign languages that you spoke _____

_____

_____

_____

Any awards you won _____

_____

_____

_____

Any organizations to which you belonged

_____

_____

_____

Any offices that you held

_____

_____

_____

_____

All the days ordained for me
were written in your book before
one of them came to be.
Psalms 139: 14, 16 NIV

Favorites
"These are a few of my favorite things"

What is your favorite:

Color _____

Song and kind of music _____

_____

Book(s) _____

Animal _____

Bird _____

Flower _____

Sport _____

Food _____

Kind of day _____

Style of furniture _____

Season _____

Holiday _____

Radio program (include a past favorite) _____

_____

Movie _____

_____

Think about things
that are pure and lovely,

What is your favorite thing to do   (sport, hobby, craft, and so on) ?

_____

_____

What was your favorite place while you were growing up?

_____

What was your favorite subject while you were in school?

_____

Who was your favorite teacher and why?

_____

_____

What was your favorite toy when you were a child?

_____

What was your favorite vacation or place you visited?

_____

_____

and dwell on the fine, good things in others...
See Philippians 4:8

What is your favorite Bible story? _____

_____

Your favorite Bible verse? _____

_____

Character from Scripture? _____

What is your favorite motto or little saying? _____

_____

What was the best gift you ever received? _____

_____

Did you have a favorite piece of clothing—something
you really enjoyed wearing or especially wanted? _____

_____

_____

What are your most prized possessions? _____

_____

_____

_____

Think about all you can praise God
for and be glad about.
Philippians 4:8 TLB

Do you have any phobias or fears?

_____

_____

What are some things you don't like to do?
(washing windows, driving in the
dark, and so on). _____

_____

_____

What are some foods you dislike? _____

_____

While you were growing up, did you have any
clothing or shoes that you didn't like wearing? _____

_____

_____

The Lord is the strength of my life;
of whom shall I be afraid?
Psalms 27:1 KJV

Firsts

Do you remember the first time you were away from home?
(Where did you go? Who did you go with? And so on). _____

_____

_____

Who was the first boy or girl
you ever had a crush on? _____

What happened? _____

_____

_____

_____

What was your first date like? (Where did you go?

Who did you go with? What time did you have to be home?) _____

_____

_____

_____

_____

_____

_____

The Lord will guard your going
out and your coming in. From this time
forth and forever.
Psalms 121:8 NAS

What was your first job interview like?
(name of business, type of job interviewed for, and so on). _____

_____

_____

What was your first job like? _____

_____

_____

_____

Did you work while attending school? _____

What kind of work did you do? _____

_____

_____

What was your employer like? _____

_____

_____

_____

_____

What was your salary then? _____

For a soul is far too precious to be
ransomed by mere earthly wealth.
Psalms 49:8 TLB

21

Describe your first big trip. _____

_____

_____

_____

How did you travel and where did you go? _____

_____

_____

_____

Do you remember your first car
or perhaps the first car your family owned? _____

How did it feel to drive your own car? _____

_____

_____

Did you pay cash for it or pay on credit? _____

The righteous shall move
onward and forward; those
with pure hearts shall become
stronger and stronger.
Job 17:9 TLB

What was the first thing you bought for yourself with your own money? _____

_____

What was the first gift you bought with your own money? _____

_____

For whom did you buy it? _____

Do you remember the first time you saw your spouse? _____

What first attracted you to him or her? _____

_____

_____

_____

_____

But seek ye first the kingdom
of God, and his righteousness;
and all these things shall be
added unto you.
Matthew 6:33 KJV

When I Was Young

I loved my uncle's ranch when I was a child.

> There was space to run unhampered
> and freedom to explore.

The dust lay inches thick upon the trails

> And running barefoot down a path of sifted powder
> was a sumptuous sort of feel.

The barn was my playground full of animated toys.

The loft was full of hay and mice and fairly friendly spiders.

The mint grew wild and plush beside the creek.

My aunt made berry pies

> and the smell would seek me out
> anywhere I played around the house.

I rode my cousin's palomino horse

> through fantasies that never seemed to end.

If I'm careful, Lord, I can edit these thoughts and forget

> that I got a bee sting when I picked the mint
> and burned my tongue time and again on the berry pies
> because I never seemed to learn and couldn't wait.
> That the barn smelled just awful
> and the horse made my bottom sore

24

and the dust that felt like sifted powder

    made me sneeze all summer.

    If I'm careful, I can forget these things.

    But, if I'm wise

        I can remember that all of life has both things in it

        and I may choose which part to hold to me.

MARILEE ZDENEK

Train up a child in the way he should go: and when he is old, he will not depart from it.

Proverbs 22:6 KJV

The greatest happiness of life is the conviction that we are loved, loved for ourselves, or rather loved in spite of ourselves.

VICTOR HUGO

We are here to help each other, to try to make each other happy.

SAYING OF THE POLAR ESKIMO

O Lord, you have examined my heart and know everything about me. You know when I sit or stand. When far away you know my every thought. You chart my path ahead of me....

Psalms 139:1–3 TLB

Did you come from another country? _____

Did your parents come from another country? _____

What was it like to come to
America, for you or for them? _____

_____

_____

_____

_____

_____

_____

He reigns above the
nations, sitting
on his holy throne.
Psalms 47:8 TLB

Were you born in the United States? _____

Did you live in the country or in a city? _____

What was your home like? _____

_____

_____

_____

Your community? _____

_____

_____

Unless the Lord builds a house,
the builders' work is useless.
Psalms 127:1 TLB

What was your room like? (name some of the things in your room). _____

_____

_____

_____

_____

_____

_____

Did you share your room? _____

In my father's house are many
rooms; if it were not so,
I would have told you....
John 14:2 NIV

What was your favorite spot at home?
(family room, kitchen, somewhere outdoors, and so on). _____

_____

What do you remember doing when you had nothing special to do? _____

_____

_____

_____

_____

In what room did your family tend to gather? _____

_____

Lord, Thou hast been our
dwelling place in all generations.
Psalms 90:1 NAS

What were your parents' names?

_____

_____

What were their occupations?

_____

_____

What were some of their outstanding characteristics?

_____

_____

_____

_____

_____

_____

A good name is rather to be chosen than great riches....

Proverbs 22:1 KJV

What were their hobbies? (some of the things they liked to do). _____

_____

_____

What illnesses did they suffer from? _____

_____

_____

What were their ages at death? _____

Where are they buried? _____

_____

_____

...Death is swallowed up in victory.
I Corinthians 15:54 KJV

How did your mother seek to comfort you? _____

_____

_____

_____

Did she sing lullabies to you? _____

What were some of the foods she cooked
that you especially enjoyed? (Include recipes, if available.) _____

_____

_____

_____

_____

_____

_____

Every wise woman buildeth
her house....
Proverbs 14:1 KJV

Did your father tell you stories? _____

What about? _____

_____

_____

_____

Were your parents strict with you? _____

How did they punish you if you disobeyed? _____

_____

_____

...the Lord disciplines those he loves, as a father the
son he delights in.
Proverbs 3:12 NIV

What are the names and birth dates of your brothers and sisters?
(If you do not know their birth dates,
write how much older or younger they were than you.)

_____

_____

_____

What were they like as people? _____

_____

_____

_____

_____

_____

_____

_____

_____

I will be a father to you, and you will be
my sons and daughters....
2 Corinthians 6:18 NIV

What were some of the times you remember having with them? _____

_____

_____

_____

_____

_____

_____

What did they become when they grew up? _____

_____

_____

_____

Where are they now? _____

_____

_____

_____

...Look not only to your own interests, but also to
the interests of others.
Philippians 2:4 NIV

What were the names of your aunts, uncles, and grandparents? _____

_____

_____

_____

_____

Did you visit them often? _____

What were some of the places you went together? _____

_____

_____

_____

_____

_____

...He cares for those who trust in him.
Nahum 1:7 NIV

What were they like as people? _____

_____

_____

_____

_____

_____

_____

_____

Who were your special favorites and why? _____

_____

_____

_____

_____

_____

_____

Each one should use whatever gift he
has received to serve others....
1 Peter 4:10 NIV

How did you spend your summer days? _____

_____

_____

_____

Your winter days? _____

_____

_____

_____

What were the chores for which you were responsible? _____

_____

_____

_____

Did you get an allowance? _____

...My Father will honor the one
who serves me.
John 12:26 NIV

Who were some of your childhood friends? _____

_____

_____

Do you still keep in touch? (Include addresses if you have them.) _____

_____

_____

_____

What were some of the games you played together? _____

_____

_____

Did you have a nickname? _____

How did you get it? _____

_____

_____

_____

For where two or three come together in my name,
there am I with them.
Matthew 18:20 NIV

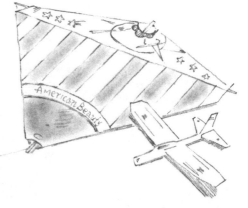

How did your family celebrate special days like birthdays, Christmas, and Easter?

_____

_____

_____

_____

_____

_____

_____

Were there certain foods or rituals your family enjoyed? _____

_____

_____

_____

_____

But may the righteous be glad and rejoice before God;
may they be happy and joyful.
Psalms 68:3 NIV

What did you enjoy doing just for fun? _____

_____

_____

_____

What did you want to be when you grew up? _____

_____

Did you ever lose something of value? What happened? _____

_____

_____

_____

_____

Did you ever find something of value? What happened then? _____

_____

_____

_____

_____

Watch and pray so that you will not
fall into temptation....
Matthew 26:41 NIV

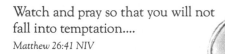

Did any of your loved ones die while you were young? _____

_____

What do you remember of that time? _____

_____

_____

_____

_____

From what did the person die? _____

_____

Is it something we can cure today? _____

_____

I give them eternal life, and they shall never
perish; no one can snatch them
out of my hand.
John 10:28 NIV

Describe the school(s) that you attended (one room or larger). _____

_____

_____

_____

Who were some of your teachers, and what were they like? _____

_____

_____

_____

_____

_____

In which subjects did you do the best?

_____

_____

In which did you have some difficulty?

_____

_____

I will instruct you and teach you
in the way you should go....
Psalms 32:8 NIV

43

In what activities were you involved? (plays, pageants, clubs, or special events). _____

_____

_____

_____

_____

Did you have class trips? Where to? _____

_____

_____

What were your major accomplishments in school? _____

_____

_____

_____

_____

_____

However, Christ has given each of us special
abilities—whatever he wants us to have
out of his rich storehouse of gifts.
Ephesians 4:7 TLB

Did you ever get in trouble in school? _____

What did you do and how were you punished? _____

_____

_____

What was your most embarrassing moment? _____

_____

What embarrassed you? _____

_____

_____

_____

_____

No discipline seems pleasant at the time, but painful. Later on, however, it produces a harvest of righteousness and peace....
Hebrews 12:11 NIV

Dunc

Cap

As a teenager, how did you feel about yourself physically? _____

_____

_____

_____

_____

Did you think you were too fat or too thin? Too tall or too short? _____

_____

_____

_____

What did you like most about yourself? Least? _____

_____

_____

_____

_____

Men judge by outward appearance, but
I look at a man's thoughts and intentions.
1 Samuel 16:7 TLB

What skills or talents were you known for then? _____

_____

_____

Did you have a hero or a heroine? _____

_____

Was it someone from a book or real life? _____

_____

Why did you admire him or her? _____

_____

_____

_____

...[God] is able to do immeasurably
more than all we ask or imagine,
according to his power that is at
work within us.

Ephesians 3:20 NIV

What teacher, book, or thoughts influenced the direction of your life the most and how?

_____

_____

_____

_____

_____

_____

_____

_____

_____

_____

_____

_____

_____

_____

It is better to listen to the rebuke of a wise man
Than for one to listen to
the song of fools.
Ecclesiastes 7:5 NAS

Did your family take you to church? _____

To Sunday school? _____

How did you get to church? (walk, streetcar, and so on). _____

_____

How was church different then? _____

_____

_____

_____

_____

_____

The fool hath said in his heart, There is no God.
Psalms 14:1 KJV

Memories

Live your life while you have it. Life is a splendid gift. There
is nothing small in it. For the greatest things grow by God's Law
out of the smallest. But to live your life you must discipline it. You
must not fritter it away in "fair purpose, erring act, inconstant will"
but make your thoughts, your acts, all work to the same end and that
end, not self but God.

FLORENCE NIGHTINGALE

The Gesture of Love

Oh, the comfort, an inexpressible comfort of feeling safe with a person;
having neither to weigh thoughts nor measure words, but to pour them all
out, just as they are, chaff and grain together, knowing that a faithful hand
will take and sift them, keep what is worth keeping, and then with the
breath of kindness, blow the rest away.

GEORGE ELIOT

The Dream

Great it is to believe the dream

When we stand in youth by the starry stream;

But a greater thing is to fight life through

And say at the end, "The dream is true!"

EDWIN MARKHAM

50

There is no more searching test of the human spirit than
the way it behaves when fortune is adverse and it has to pass
through a prolonged period of disappointing failures. Then comes
the real proof of the man. Achievement, if a man has the ability, is a
joy; but to take hard knocks and come up smiling, to have your main-
sail blown away and then rig a sheet on the bowsprit and sail on—this is
perhaps the deepest test of character.

HARRY EMERSON FOSDICK

I love you not only for what you are,

but for what I am when I am with you.

I love you not only for what you have made of yourself,

but for what you are making of me.

ROY CROFT

Commit your work to the Lord, then it will succeed.

Proverbs 16:3 TLB

Love forgets mistakes; nagging about them parts the best of friends.

Proverbs 17:9 TLB

How did you meet your marriage partner? _____

_____

_____

_____

_____

_____

What did you most admire about him or her? _____

_____

_____

_____

_____

_____

_____

What were some of the things you did during your courtship?
(places you visited, transportation you used, and so on).

_____

_____

_____

_____

_____

_____

LOVES ME ME NOT

Love is very patient and kind, never jealous or envious....
1 Corinthians 13:4 TLB

What was the date of your wedding? _____

What was your wedding like? _____

_____

_____

_____

_____

What size was it? _____

_____

_____

Where was it held? _____

Was there a reception? _____

What did you wear? _____

_____

_____

What did your mate wear? _____

_____

Your attendants? _____

_____

_____

Did you go on a honeymoon? _____

If so, where? _____

_____

...Love does not demand its own way...If
you love someone you will be loyal to
him no matter what the cost....
1 Corinthians 13:5, 7 TLB

Where did you first live after you were married?
(with parents, in an apartment, and so on). _____

_____

_____

When were you able to purchase a house? _____

_____

What was your first home like? _____

_____

_____

_____

_____

What did it cost to purchase a house then? _____

...Be patient with each other, making
allowance for each other's faults
because of your love.
Ephesians 4:2 TLB

What were some of the problems you faced together?

_____

_____

_____

_____

What were some of the difficult adjustments you had to make?

_____

_____

_____

_____

_____

What helped you most in facing difficulties?

_____

_____

_____

_____

_____

_____

_____

Don't worry about anything; instead, pray
about everything; tell God your needs and
don't forget to thank him for his answers.
Philippians 4:6 TLB

PINCH

PENNIES

Where did you go on your vacations and trips?

_____

_____

_____

_____

_____

What was the best trip you ever took?

_____

_____

_____

_____

_____

Did you have a place you went to regularly for vacations?

_____

_____

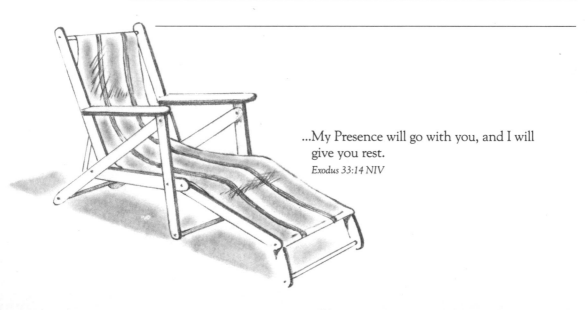

...My Presence will go with you, and I will
give you rest.
Exodus 33:14 NIV

Who were some of the friends you enjoyed as a couple?

_____

_____

_____

What things did you like to do together? _____

_____

_____

_____

Do you still keep in touch? _____

What were some of the games you played?

_____

_____

_____

Some of the books you read?

_____

_____

_____

Before television, what did you do for recreation in the evening?

_____

_____

_____

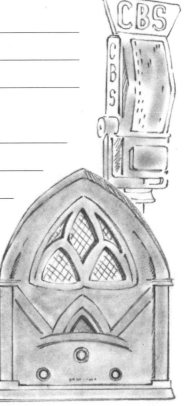

Let no debt remain outstanding, except the
continuing debt to love another....
Romans 13:8 NIV

What are your children's names?

_____

_____

_____

_____

_____

What are their birth dates?

_____

_____

_____

_____

_____

What are the unique qualities of each one?

_____

_____

_____

_____

_____

_____

_____

_____

For I have chosen him, so that he will direct his
children and his household after him to keep the
way of the Lord by doing what is right and just....
Genesis 18:19 NIV

What are some of the little stories you remember about their childhoods?
(funny things they said or did, times they got into trouble).

_____

_____

_____

_____

_____

_____

_____

_____

_____

_____

_____

_____

_____

_____

_____

May the Lord make your love increase and
overflow for each other and for everyone else....
1 Thessalonians 3:12 NIV

What are some stories from their teenage years?

_____

_____

_____

_____

_____

_____

_____

_____

_____

_____

_____

List some of their qualities you take pride in.

_____

_____

_____

_____

_____

_____

The glory of young men is their strength;
of old men, their experience.
Proverbs 20:29 TLB

What was a typical income then? _____

What did automobiles cost? Clothing? _____

_____

_____

What were some of your favorite stores? _____

_____

_____

_____

_____

What lines of merchandise did they carry? _____

_____

_____

_____

_____

Are these brands still available today? _____

_____

But remember the Lord your God, for
it is he who gives you the ability
to produce wealth....
Deuteronomy 8:18 NIV

What was a routine day like at your job? _____

_____

_____

_____

What was your position called? _____

If you worked outside your home, what time did you have to leave for work? _____

What transportation did you use to get there?

_____

_____

Who were some of your friends at work?

_____

_____

_____

If you had several careers or jobs, why did you leave one and move to another?

_____

_____

_____

_____

_____

...walk worthy of the vocation
wherewith ye are called.
Ephesians 4:1 KJV

What did you most enjoy about your life work? _____

_____

_____

_____

What were your greatest rewards? Greatest challenges? _____

_____

_____

_____

_____

_____

Would you have done anything different if you could have done so? _____

_____

_____

_____

_____

_____

_____

_____

_____

_____

And God is able to make all grace abound to you, so that
in all things at all times, having all that you need, you
will abound in every good work.

2 Corinthians 9:8 NIV

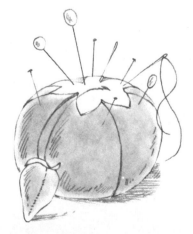

What was the name of your family doctor?

_____

What was some of his best advice to you? _____

_____

_____

If you had to go to the hospital, did you have a long stay? _____

Were there any problems or complications? _____

_____

Did you suffer from any serious illnesses? _____

_____

_____

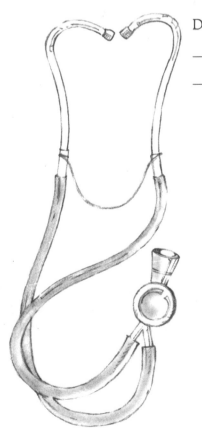

Did other members of your family? _____

_____

_____

A merry heart doeth good like a medicine....
Proverbs 17:22 KJV

What was your neighborhood like? Your neighbors? _____

_____

_____

_____

_____

_____

_____

Were some of them close friends? _____

_____

_____

Were there stores in your neighborhood that you could walk to? _____

_____

_____

_____

...He is our God and we are the
people of his pasture, the flock
under his care.
Psalms 95:7 NIV

In the Course of a Lifetime

In this world you had no choice over many lines in
your pattern. You did not choose your era of birth,
your country, family, social status. You did not
choose your form, abilities, limitations. These I
choose.

But you ARE choosing your heavenly pattern.
You will be rewarded or suffer loss as you invest the
gifts and talents I have given you.

Far more.

As you choose to respond or react to the
circumstances, to the people I send in life, you
choose what you shall be and what you shall
possess through all eternity.

From *Parables by the Sea*
PAMELA REEVE

Thou that hast given so much to me,
Give one thing more—a grateful heart.

GEORGE HERBERT

What is faith? It is the confident assurance that
something we want is going to happen.

Hebrews 11:1 TLB

If I can stop one heart from breaking,

I shall not live in vain;

If I can ease one life the aching,

Or cool one pain,

Or help one fainting robin

Unto his nest again,

I shall not live in vain.

EMILY DICKINSON

Why should we think about things that are lovely?
Because thinking determines life. It is a common
mistake to blame life upon environment.
Environment modifies but does not govern life. The
soul is stronger than its surroundings.

WILLIAM JAMES

Looking back over your life, for what things are you most thankful?

_____

_____

_____

_____

_____

_____

_____

_____

_____

_____

_____

_____

_____

_____

_____

_____

_____

As for God, his way is perfect; the word
of the Lord is flawless....
2 Samuel 22:31 NIV

What people influenced your life the most and how? _____

_____

_____

_____

_____

_____

_____

_____

_____

What was the best advice you ever received? _____

_____

_____

_____

_____

_____

_____

_____

_____

Ask and it will be given to you; seek and
you will find; knock and the door
will be opened to you.
Matthew 7:7 NIV

In your opinion, what good things have we lost to progress?

_____

_____

_____

_____

_____

What current trends in society make you the most hopeful? The most disturbed?

_____

_____

_____

_____

_____

_____

_____

_____

_____

_____

For I am the Lord, I change not....
Malachi 3:6 KJV

What was the most difficult problem you ever had to face? _____

_____

_____

_____

_____

_____

What was the most difficult time you had to live through?
(fire, flood, hurricane, famine, plague, war, and so on). _____

_____

_____

How did you manage? _____

_____

_____

_____

_____

_____

_____

_____

_____

_____

And even the very hairs of your head are
numbered. So don't be afraid; you
are worth more than many sparrows.
Matthew 10:30, 31 NIV

What decision most influenced the direction of your life? _____

_____

_____

_____

_____

How did you arrive at this decision? _____

_____

_____

_____

_____

_____

_____

Did you have a formula for making decisions? _____

_____

_____

_____

Trust in the Lord with all your
heart and lean not on
your own understanding....
Proverbs 3:5 NIV

What decisions would you have liked to change?

_____

_____

_____

_____

_____

_____

Are there some things you wish you could have done? (places you would have liked to have visited, and so on).

_____

_____

_____

_____

_____

_____

_____

_____

_____

Lord, if you keep in mind our sins then who can ever get an answer to his prayers? But you forgive! What an awesome thing this is!
Psalms 130:3, 4 TLB

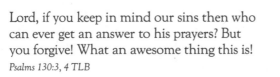

What was your greatest disappointment in life?

_____

_____

_____

_____

_____

_____

_____

_____

_____

_____

_____

_____

_____

_____

_____

_____

Wherefore seeing we also are compassed about
with so great a cloud of witnesses, let us
lay aside every weight, and the sin which
doth so easily beset us....
Hebrews 12:1 KJV

What were your greatest successes?

_____

_____

_____

_____

_____

_____

_____

_____

_____

_____

_____

_____

_____

_____

_____

_____

_____

_____

...And let us run with patience the race that is set before us.
Hebrews 12:1 KJV

Our Spirits Never Die

Grow old along with me!
The best is yet to be,
The last of life, for which the first was made:
Our times are in his hand
Who saith "A whole I planned,
Youth shows but half; trust God:
see all, nor be afraid!"

ROBERT BROWNING

Yea, though I walk through the valley of the shadow
of death, I will fear no evil: for thou art with me....

Psalms 23:4 KJV

Oh the sheer joy of it
Ever to be
Living in glory,
Living with Thee,
Lord of tomorrow,
Lover of me!

RALPH SPAULDING CUSHMAN

In Thine Own Heart

Though Christ a thousand times

In Bethlehem be born,

If he's not born in thee

Thy soul is still forlorn.

The cross on Golgotha

Will never save thy soul,

The cross in thine own heart

Alone can make thee whole.

ANGELUS SILESIUS

Let not your heart be troubled. You are trusting God, now trust in me. There are many homes up there where my Father lives, and I am going to prepare them for your coming. When everything is ready, then I will come and get you, so that you can always be with me where I am....

John 14:1–3 TLB

We have the promises of God as thick as daisies in summer meadows, that death, which men most fear, shall be to us the most blessed of experiences, if we trust in Him. Death is unclasping; joy breaking out in the desert; the heart coming to its blossoming time! Do we call it dying when the bud bursts into flower?

HENRY WARD BEECHER

When and how did you come to realize God's great love
for you and that salvation is a free gift through Jesus Christ? _____

_____

_____

_____

_____

_____

_____

_____

_____

_____

_____

_____

_____

_____

_____

_____

_____

_____

_____

Because of his kindness you have been saved
through trusting Christ. And even trusting
is not of yourselves; it too is a gift
from God.

Ephesians 2:8 TLB

Over your lifetime, what Scriptures have meant the most to you?

_____

_____

_____

_____

_____

_____

_____

_____

Were there promises or assurances that you found particularly helpful?

_____

_____

_____

_____

_____

_____

_____

_____

_____

_____

Salvation is not a reward for the good
we have done, so none of us can
take any credit for it.
Ephesians 2:9 TLB

What prayers of yours have been answered in a dramatic way?

_____

_____

_____

_____

_____

_____

_____

_____

_____

_____

_____

_____

_____

_____

_____

_____

...Ask, using my name, and you will
receive, and your cup of joy
will overflow.
John 16:24 TLB

If you could give your family
anything, what would it be? _____

_____

_____

_____

_____

_____

_____

_____

_____

What do you include in your prayers for your family? _____

_____

_____

_____

_____

_____

_____

_____

_____

_____

_____

_____

_____

My prayer for you is that you will overflow
more and more with love for others....
Philippians 1:9 TLB

What are the most important values you wish you could pass on?

_____

_____

_____

_____

_____

_____

Which lessons that you have learned would you like to share with your loved ones?

_____

_____

_____

_____

_____

_____

_____

_____

_____

For if we are faithful to the end,...
we will share in all that belongs
to Christ.
Hebrews 3:14 TLB

What advice would you offer to a family member facing
the death of a loved one? _____

_____

_____

_____

_____

_____

_____

What helped you most when facing such a loss? _____

_____

_____

_____

_____

_____

_____

_____

_____

_____

_____

_____

So our aim is to please him always in everything we do,
whether we are here in this body...or with him in heaven.
2 Corinthians 5:9 TLB

What would you like to tell your loved one about:

Choosing a marriage partner?

_____

_____

_____

_____

_____

_____

_____

_____

Making a marriage work?

_____

_____

_____

_____

_____

_____

_____

_____

_____

In response to all he has done for us, let us outdo each other in being helpful and kind to each other and in doing good.
Hebrews 10:24 TLB

What would you share about:

Choosing a home and its upkeep?

_____

_____

_____

_____

_____

_____

_____

_____

Keeping friends?

_____

_____

_____

_____

_____

_____

_____

_____

_____

_____

Keep your eyes on Jesus, our leader
and instructor....
Hebrews 12:2 TLB

What did you learn about:

Making a success of a career?

_____
_____
_____
_____
_____
_____
_____
_____

Raising a family?

_____
_____
_____
_____
_____
_____
_____
_____

Don't be misled; remember that you can't ignore
God...a man will always reap just the kind
of crop he sows!
Galatians 6:7 TLB

Describe the insights you have concerning retirement years.

_____

_____

_____

_____

_____

_____

_____

_____

_____

_____

_____

_____

_____

_____

Teach us to number our days and recognize how few
they are; help us to spend them as we should.
Psalms 90:12 TLB

Do you feel afraid to grow old? To die? _____

_____

How has Jesus helped you with this fear? _____

_____

_____

_____

_____

_____

How would you tell your loved ones they may
have security in facing death and the life to come? _____

_____

_____

_____

_____

_____

_____

_____

_____

_____

_____

For to me, living means opportunities for Christ,
and dying—well, that's better yet!...for I long to
go and be with Christ....

Philippians 1:21, 23 TLB

What do you believe is the most important thing in all the world?

_____

_____

_____

_____

_____

_____

_____

_____

_____

_____

_____

_____

_____

_____

_____

_____

_____

_____

_____

_____

Thank God for his Son—his Gift too
wonderful for words.

2 Corinthians 9:15 TLB

Are there any other things you
would like to tell your loved ones?

_____

_____

_____

_____

_____

_____

_____

_____

_____

_____

_____

_____

_____

_____

_____

_____

So, my dear brothers, since future victory is sure, be strong
and steady, always abounding in the Lord's work, for you
know that nothing you do for the Lord is ever wasted
as it would be if there were no resurrection.

I Corinthians 15:58 TLB

your name

brothers & sisters
names

_____
_____
_____
_____

mother's name

father's name

Family
Tree

mother's brothers & sisters name

_____
_____
_____

father's brothers & sisters names

_____
_____

grandmother

grandfather

grandfather

grandmother

great-grandparents

great-grandparents

great-grandparents

great-grandparents

Every man's life is a plan of God.
HORACE BUSHNELL

Photos and Mementos